MOLA

CUNA LIFE STORIES AND ART

MARICEL E. PRESILLA

HENRY HOLT AND COMPANY · NEW YORK

Acknowledgments

The Cuna like to talk about their history and traditions. I was lucky to find generous, learned people in the San Blas Islands who were eager to share their lives and stories with me. I am indebted to the following: Luis Burgos of the island of Nalunega for being such a good storyteller; his grandson Juan Amado Iglesias, a skilled sailor and the most unusual guide one could ever hope to find; *argar* José Davies, for believing in the importance of history and for being the keeper of the old ways on his island of Cartí Sugdupu; his son Delfino Davies for being as strong as the Igua tree in his defense of Cuna tradition; Demetrio López of Nalunega for his beautiful chanting; the daughters of the late Sia Bipi for singing "Dolin Dolin Dosa," my favorite Cuna song; Griselda García, for her independent spirit and her tasty lobster; Manuel González and his young bride for letting me record their wedding; and Ermelina Hernández, Siaquaru Fernández, and Marbelin Martínez for elevating mola making to the finest art. My thanks to Flory Saltzman in Panama and my friends, New York mola collectors Jacques Carcanaques and Sergio Francescon, and to Alejandro Presilla for braving storms and pirates to photograph the Cuna paradise. Lullabies on pages 14, 15, and 20 were recorded and translated by ethnomusicologist Sandra Smith McCoster. Used by permission of the Gothenburg Ethnographical Museum, Sweden.

Henry Holt and Company, Inc.
Publishers since 1866
115 West 18th Street
New York, New York 10011
Henry Holt is a registered trademark of
Henry Holt and Company, Inc.
Copyright © 1996 by Maricel E. Presilla
All rights reserved.
Published in Canada by Fitzhenry & Whiteside Ltd.,
195 Allstate Parkway, Markham, Ontario L3R 4T8.

Library of Congress Cataloging-in-Publication Data
Presilla, Maricel E. Mola: Cuna life stories and art / by Maricel E. Presilla;
molas by the Cuna women of the San Blas Islands of Panama.
1. Cuna women—Costume—Juvenile literature. 2. Cuna women—Industries—
Juvenile literature. 3. Molas—Panama—San Blas Islands—Juvenile literature.
4. Cuna textile fabrics—Panama—San Blas Islands—Juvenile literature.
5. San Blas Islands (Panama)—Social life and customs. I. Title.
F1565.2.C8P68 1996 305.48'8982—dc20 95-46397
ISBN 0-8050-3801-9
First Edition—1996
Printed in the United States of America on acid-free paper. ∞
10 9 8 7 6 5 4 3 2 1

For my father,
ISMAEL ESPINOSA,
with gratitude for teaching me to love the
colors of an island and to see beyond them

To the industrious Cuna women, stitchers of
Technicolor dreams, for proudly wearing their lives

ALEJANDRO PRESILLA

ALEJANDRO PRESILLA

YOUNG GIRL FROM
THE ISLAND OF THE PECCARY
(CARTÍ YANTUPO)

GRANDMOTHER FROM
THE ISLAND OF THE PELICAN
(CORBISKI)

▢▢▢▢▢▢▢▢▢▢▢▢▢▢▢▢▢▢▢▢▢▢

A long and narrow strip of land joins Central and South America. It is the Isthmus of Panama, a place of thick forests and swampy marshes hugged by the Caribbean Sea and the Pacific Ocean.

Every weekday at the crack of dawn, tiny airplanes leave Panama City and cross the isthmus, heading toward the rising sun. The planes fly above dense, dark forests. Once in a while, when slivers of moon peep through the heavy clouds, the streams and rivers that cut through the forest shine like a silvery spider's web. But as the first rays of sun pierce the darkness, a big splash of blue suddenly gleams on the horizon. Everyone in the plane looks out the windows to catch a first sight of the beautiful San Blas Islands.

From the air, these islands seem no bigger than jellyfish floating lazily in the shiny turquoise and cobalt blue waters of the Caribbean Sea. But as the plane descends, the floating shapes turn into sandy islands crowned by slender coconut trees.

Strung along the Caribbean coast of Panama, the San Blas Islands are the home of the remarkable Cuna Indians.

But the Cuna have not always lived on islands. In 1513, when the Spanish explorer Vasco Núñez de Balboa first crossed the isthmus and saw the Pacific Ocean, Cuna villages dotted the mainland.

Today, a portrait of Balboa wearing a metal helmet can be seen on the coins of Panama and in the colorful molas, or blouses, of the Cuna women.

Why was our land taken away from us?
Why couldn't we be free?
We wish our fathers had been free like birds;
We want to be free as birds, as a bird's song.

— CUNA SONG "DOLIN DOLIN DOSA," SUNG BY SIA BIPI'S
DAUGHTERS OF THE ISLAND OF CARTÍ SUGDUPU

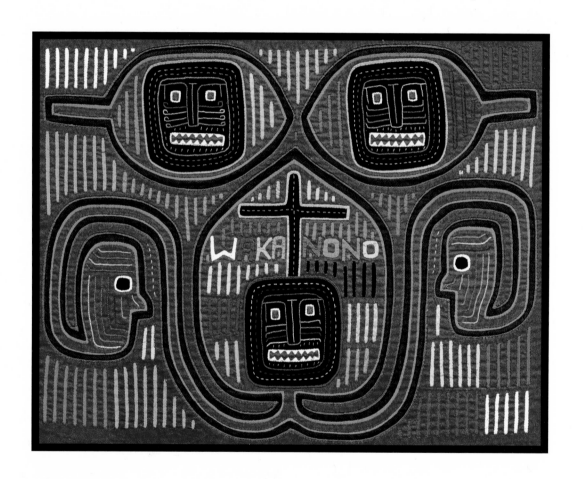

The Cuna fought the Spaniards fiercely for control of the mainland. Storytellers say that on a beach known as Waka Nono, or the Place of the Strangers' Heads, the Cuna killed hundreds of Spaniards. Then they cut off their heads and threw them into the sea. But even that could not hold back the invaders.

△▽△▽△▽△ ▽△▽△ △▽△▽△▽△ ▽△▽ △ ▽△▽ △ ▽△▽△▽△▽△ ▽△▽ △ ▽△▽ △ ▽△▽△▽△▽△

About 150 years ago, the Cuna set out to sea in dugout canoes called *cayucos* to escape from the Spaniards and their descendants, the Panamanian *criollos*. They did not have to go very far. The San Blas Islands offered them a safe haven where they could build villages and raise their families.

Every day, Cuna men paddle their *cayucos* to the mainland to tend their fields. When they are done, they bring back precious firewood and barrels filled with river water for their villages.

The Cuna are governed by three *caciques*, or chieftains, who meet in front of great general assemblies to discuss the problems that affect their communities.

Each island also has its own leaders, or *sahilas*. The *sahilas* meet with their people in what they call congress halls. They lie down in their hammocks and smoke pipes or cigarettes, then they chant in a special language no one else understands. The *argars*, or speakers, sit next to the hammocks and interpret the *sahilas*'s words for everyone.

The sahila *sings all night, then the* argar *says, "Tekie, that's the way it was." But if we fall asleep, there comes a Cuna policeman, and he shouts in a loud voice, "Listen well, do not fall asleep," and he scares everybody and wakes us up. And the* argar *says when the* sahila *stops speaking, "Tekie, that's the way it was."*

—DEMETRIO LÓPEZ OF THE ISLAND OF NALUNEGA

Today, primary schools established by the Panamanian government on the main islands teach the Cuna Indians to speak and write Spanish. Though the islands are semi-independent, the Cuna are citizens of Panama and have the rights and duties of all Panamanians.

It is easy to recognize a primary school in the San Blas Islands. While most Cuna houses are palm-thatched wooden huts, schools are built with cement blocks. The islands are usually very hot, but the schools remain cool and comfortable as sea breezes blow through the blocks. The school on the island of Wichubwuala has a faucet with running water beside the front door. The red-and-blue flag of Panama flies over its roof.

△▽△▽△▽△ ▽△▽△ ▽△▽△▽△▽△ ▽△▽ ▽△▽△▽△▽△▽△▽△ ▽△▽△▽△▽

When the boys grow up
They will fish far out to sea
Mama will eat their fish

—LULLABY, LETICIA FERNÁNDEZ OF NALUNEGA

When the Cuna men are not working their fields on the mainland or tending their coconut plantations on the islands, they go fishing. The Caribbean waters teem with sweet-tasting spiny lobsters, red snappers, and swordfish. Sharks and the feared manta ray, which the Cuna call the devilfish, also patrol the island waters. The Cuna catch sharks and manta rays to sell but do not eat them.

You are still young girls and mama is happy
Happy that you are already older
You are old enough to cook and wash the clothes of the visitors. . . .
You will always be happy
Happy since you are women

—LULLABY, ANGÉLICA BURGOS OF NALUNEGA

Cuna women stay at home and perform many chores. They sweep the sand floors of their wooden huts clean. They go to the pier and fetch the water that the men have brought from the mainland in their *cayucos,* bucket by bucket. And they feed the family pig.

The women make a savory mash with a type of banana known as a plantain. These tasty fruits are grown by the men on the mainland. First the women peel the plantains and boil them in water. Then they place the cooked plantains in a large wooden mortar and mash them to a pulp with a heavy pestle.

Cuna women cook in a separate hut called a *sokakka*. To make a fire, they place large logs in a cross shape. Older women light the wood fires and keep them alive with straw fans. The cooking pots rest on three stones. When the women want to barbecue fish, they set a grill over the stones.

▽△▽△▽△▽△ ▽△▽△ ▽△▽△▽ ▽△▽△▽△ ▽△▽△▽△▽△▽△▽△▽△ ▽△▽△▽▽△▽

Women are the center of Cuna life. When a young woman is ready to get married, she selects her husband, who is kidnapped by both of their relatives and brought to the girl's home. When a young man marries, he must live with his wife in the house of his mother-in-law. Property is passed to children by their mothers.

Dressed in colorful clothing, the Cuna women resemble tropical birds. Their arms and legs are decked with bands of beads. In their noses they wear gold rings. Their heads are covered with long orange scarves, and their blouses are adorned with designs that tell much about their lives.

For us, the Cuna, the earth is the mother. The mountain is the mother, our mother. Nature, the forest—as well as the earth—is a woman, not a man. The mother loves us, she helps us cultivate sugarcane, cacao, and all kinds of fruits. And then comes the mother who takes care of us in the home. She also gives us good advice.

—DELFINO DAVIES (IGUADOQUIÑA)
OF CARTÍ SUGDUPU

In the month of December, the Cuna celebrate Earth Day, which they call El Día de la Madre, Mother's Day. For the Cuna, the earth is caring and generous, like a Cuna mother. On El Día de la Madre, Cuna mothers cook special meals for their children.

▽△▽△▽△▽△▽△▽△▽△▽△▽△▽△▽△▽△▽△▽△▽△▽△▽△▽△▽△

My little girls,
You will grow up and marry a grown boy.
You will grow up....
When you are married, your mama will eat fish with you;
For my daughters I will look for molas,
Molas for the little girls.

—LULLABY, LETICIA FERNÁNDEZ OF NALUNEGA

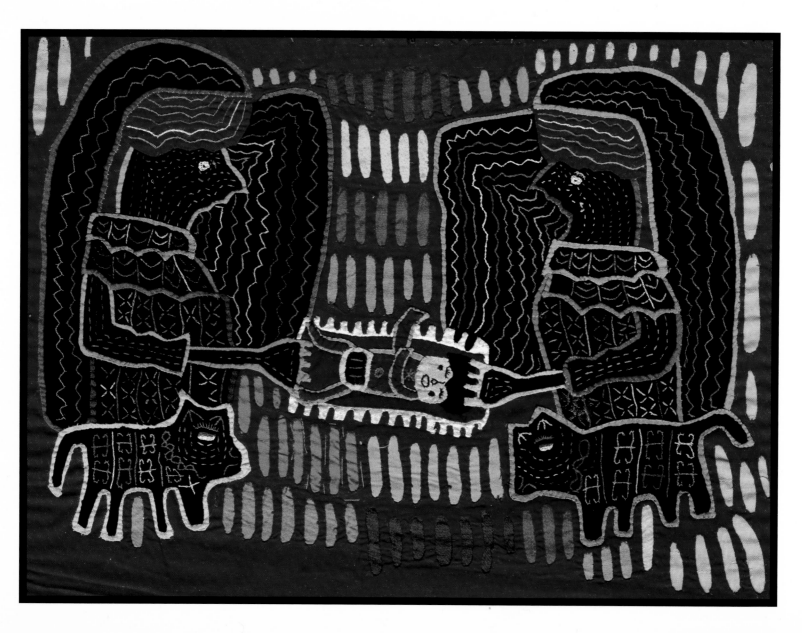

From the day they are born, Cuna girls are considered special by their families. They are lavished with gifts and attention. After all, they will bring money and respect to their families by making molas.

Cuna women are famous for their colorful blouses, called molas. Whenever a Cuna woman has some free time, she immediately gets busy sewing a mola. Whether sitting on a chair or lying in a hammock, a Cuna woman always finds time to work on a mola.

Outside the San Blas Islands, molas are often seen framed and displayed on walls as works of art. But for the Cuna women, molas are the most important part of their dress. What outsiders know as molas are the panels that adorn the front and back of a Cuna woman's blouse.

Each panel is made of many rectangular pieces of fabric of different colors and textures sewn together. Master mola maker Ermelinda Hernández of the island of Cartí Mulatupo learned to sew molas from her aunts. Some of her most beautiful molas, such as Noah's Ark, took her as long as a year to complete.

Ermelinda first draws a design on paper. Then she transfers it to the first layer of fabric. Like a sculptor, she begins to cut slits through the layers with scissors to allow different colors to show through. As she cuts, she has to stitch together the borders of the fabric. In Ermelinda's fine molas, the stitches are hardly visible.

Cuna women are observant and curious, and their molas depict many things—nature, their traditions and legends, and their daily lives. Sometimes even their dreams are told in the colorful language of a mola.

A young woman from Cartí Mulatupo once had a dream. She saw herself floating through the night sky. A gentle breeze carried her high above the mountains of the mainland. As soon as she woke up, she started working on her dream mola.

The Cuna tell their children that babies are brought to the world on the backs of animals like this giant bird.

The Panamanian mainland is home to many wild animals.
Sometimes the women paddle there to get fresh water and fruit.
On their way to the river, they see baby lizards wriggle out of their nests. Tropical birds fly overhead, and parrots perched on trees curiously watch the women as they go back to their *cayucos*. Meanwhile, large land tortoises hide in the underbrush, waiting for the women to leave.

At night, the women fall asleep in their hammocks listening to the music of the waves, for the sea is their garden.

While the Cuna sleep, owls watch over the thick mainland forests. On the islands dogs and cats guard against mice and evil spirits.

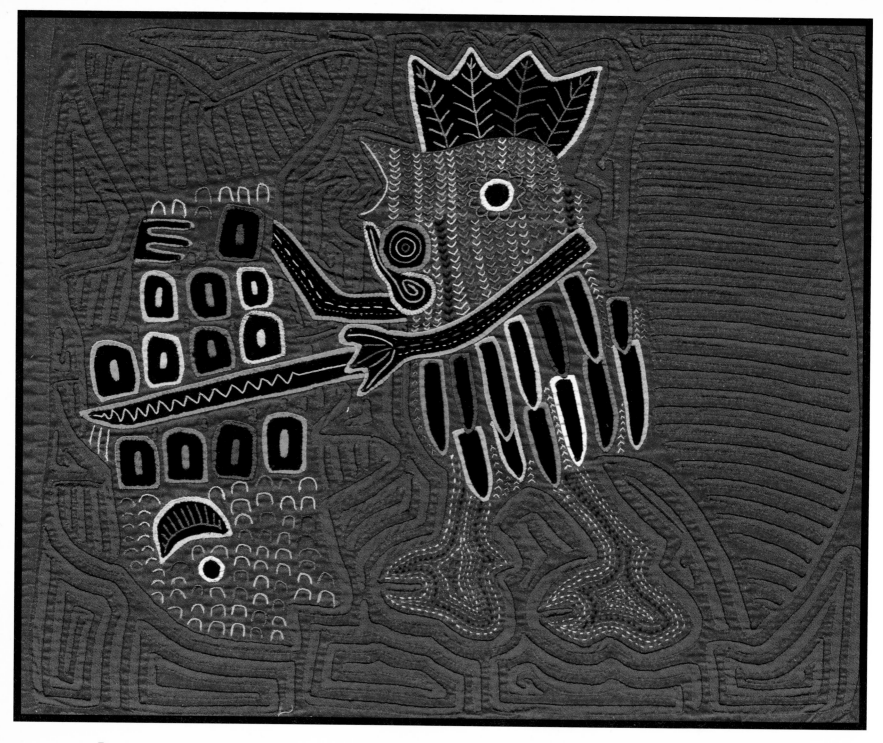

In many Cuna stories, animals act like human beings. Here a rooster is being a fisherman. He is scaling a large fish with a machete to get it ready for supper.

Cuna legends tell of a gigantic flood, as in the Bible. The Cuna's Noah was named Aiban. From the rising waters, he saved rain forest animals such as parrots, frogs, land tortoises, and wild pigs.

Cuna women are proud of their molas, and they wear the best ones on special occasions, such as the great *Inna* feast, which celebrates the coming-of-age of a young girl.

After private religious ceremonies, the Cuna gather at the congress hall for one night. They celebrate by drinking a strong liquor called *chicha fuerte* in Spanish and *inna* in Cuna. *Inna* is made with fermented sugarcane juice and corn. During this feast known as *Innamutiki,* men and women dance in circles around professional singers called *kantules.* The *kantules* chant sacred verses and play panpipes and gourd rattles.

When the Cuna girl is ready to marry, her hair is cut short and the *Inna* ceremony continues for five days and nights. Then she can take her place in the unique society of the people of the mola, the women who wear their lives.

One dark, moonless night I was riding the waves of the Caribbean Sea somewhere between the islands of Nalunega and Carti Tupile. I was aboard a blue *cayuco* piloted by José Amado, my Cuna guide. We were running late because I had spent hours talking about molas with Siaquaru Fernández, a famed octogenarian mola maker. I was trying to convince her to sell me a stunning mola showing a nest of lizards. Tiny raindrops and rolling thunder announced an imminent downpour, and we rushed onward, against the wind and the current, heading toward a flickering light on the horizon. Holding my precious cache of molas and drenched with seawater, I realized how much molas had come to mean to me over the years.

In the same blue *cayuco*, I went to the mainland to see the Cuna fields and cemeteries. While on the islands, I saw, photographed, and recorded the Cuna women as they worked, sewed, and took care of their families. On a visit to Carti Sugtupu I discovered a tiny museum dedicated to Cuna history and folklore. The curator of the collection, the *argar* José Davies, gave me a written chronicle of Cuna life and a history of his island. *Mola* is drawn from such personal encounters, as well as from wide reading in anthropological literature.

After meeting the Cuna, I could no longer see molas as only beautiful art. Now I know them as the living record of people I admire. Molas are a testament to the Cuna's creativity and ability to adapt. When they lived on the mainland, they decorated their bodies with natural pigments. After they moved to the islands, they learned to make new use of these skills by creating molas.

Molas were first crafted at the turn of the century. Since then, mola making has continued to evolve. While the designs of old molas are mostly abstract, contemporary molas depict a vast range of subjects, from scenes of daily life and mythological themes to Bugs Bunny and the space shuttle.

Because the best molas command such high prices, mola making buttresses the powerful position of the Cuna women in their matriarchal society. Molas are both beautiful art objects that tourists and serious collectors buy and records of the vibrant traditions that the Cuna women carry on today.